Otherwise Poems

by Oscar Mandel

PROSPECT
·PARK·
BOOKS

Published by Prospect Park Books
2359 Lincoln Avenue
Altadena, CA 91001
www.prospectparkbooks.com

Distributed by Consortium Book Sales & Distribution
www.cbsd.com

Library of Congress Cataloging in Publication information is on file with the Library of Congress. The following is for reference only:

Otherwise poems / Oscar Mandell
p. cm.
I. Title.
ISBN 978-1-938849-55-8

Cover design by Brad Norr.
Layout by Amy Inouye, Future Studio.
Printed in the United States of America.

For Adriana, the blessing on my life

NON-FICTION
A Definition of Tragedy
The Book of Elaborations
Fundamentals of the Art of Poetry
Etre ou ne pas être juif

TRANSLATIONS
AND CRITICAL STUDIES
Philoctetes and the Fall of Troy
The Theatre of Don Juan
Five Comedies of Medieval France
The Ariadne of Thomas Corneille
Seven Comedies by Marivaux
Prosper Mérimée: Plays on Hispanic Themes
August von Kotzebue: the Comedy, the Man
The Land of Upside Down (LudwigTieck)

ART HISTORY
The Art of Alessandro Magnasco:
an Essay in the Recovery of Meaning
The Cheerfulness of Dutch Art: a Rescue Operation

Table of Contents

TWO: BUSY EROS

THREE: NAMES

FOUR: POEMS WITH ANIMALS

FIVE: TENEBRAE

SIX: TORPORS AND DIMINUTIONS

SEVEN: THE POET

EIGHT: POEMS IN FRENCH

Foreword

Blessed by the Muse are the poets who beget volume after volume of poems for the happiness of mankind. I have only one, the present *Otherwise Poems*, but it is one that has been evolving over much of my life. Three earlier stages were fixed in print in *Simplicities* in 1974, *Collected Lyrics and Epigrams* in 1981, and *Where Is the Light?* in 2006; they were always the one-and-only book growing up. The adding, removing, modifying, refining never ceased, and they have continued as recently as last night, so to speak. However, the mortality of man decrees that *Otherwise Poems* must be the *terminus*. I thought, in fact, that *The Final Word* would be the aptest title for this little book, but better heads felt it to be too gloomy.

Because of that persistent process of addition, deletion, revision and refinement, chronology falls into a blur. What is the true date of a poem written in 1960, revised in 1990 and again reworked in 2010? Is it an early, middle or late poem? Evidently all three. In response, I have arranged my poems by topics, though rather loosely, not by year of composition or publication. All manner of other arrangements would have suited the poems as well.

Here I reproduce a few words from the preface to my 1981 volume:

"If early and late are made good neighbors in this book, so are contrary moods and notions. A book of poems is not a philosophical tract, where the writer, having thought his way past pits and boulders, reaches at last a level assurance. A book of poems is allowed to mark the pits and boulders; it is even allowed to mark nothing else and never reach any destination at all. Poems are not improved by being consistent with each other." And I quoted Wallace Stevens, to the effect that each poem is the "cry of its occasion." All this remains evidently true.

While I do not pretend that all my poems, in their varied moods and notions, are "easy to understand", I have always hoped to be intelligible to the intelligent; a hope nourished by the cheerful expectation that admirable poems that speak and sing nakedly will continue to live at peace alongside those others, dominant today, in which fragments of speech, private allusions, enigmatic gaps, mysterious collages, pregnant spaces between words or lines and other cunning operations bring about their own wonderful results, but which mask the limpid thought-filled intelligibility I want. This is the first difference from the trend which, in my opinion, justifies the title *Otherwise Poems*.

Poets of both schools have at hand many "weapons" by means of which they are able to strike pleasure into their readers. I reviewed these at leisure in my *Fundamentals of the Art of Poetry*. As even children know, among these weapons, or tools, or means, or devices, or qualities, are rhythm and rhyme. They were for ages the chief poetic weapons wielded, pen in hand, by the poets of our Western cultures. They are so no longer of course. The old confident beat of

The roll, the rise, the carol, the creation

has bowed to the democratic slouch of

Oh yes, and my laundry number,
597.

Nor is rhyme doing better than fighting a rear-guard action against slouching unrhymed verse. To be sure, free verse has beckoned to me when it seemed to me that the matter truly wanted it, but my love of music-in-poetry has remained steadfast, and at every stage of my life I have instinctively expressed my thoughts in their very strong feelings (often sardonic) through a confident verbal music without sounding, I hope, like a left-over Victorian bard. I take this pervasive music to be the second justification for the *Otherwise* in my title.

With a few exceptions, my notes to the poems are personal, beyond the reach of the most astute search engines. In my 2006 collection, wishing as always to be limpid, I identified historical persons, places and events in footnotes, but nowadays a few taps of the finger on an electronic device will do the job as well and better for the reader who may be unfamiliar with one or another fruit of what I call, in one of my poems, my sophomoric erudition.

One: Places

I have arranged the poems in this section in a sequence of places and not of subject matter, mood, form, or date of original composition; and although the poems were evoked or provoked by places, they do not necessarily intend to describe them. They begin with a cup of Italian coffee which I was happy to find in Chelsea in 1956 and terminate in a dream of anyhow indescribable paradise.

AN ESPRESSO AT THE 'NUMBER SIX'
(London 1956)

Disinherited but dignified,
alone to the right, the same to the left,
I sip my sweetened espresso
this tolerable night.

I'm thirty, and where is home?
One more year, one more roof and soul.
A man of many homes has none:
I call no spot of earth my own.

This sterling English I bagged like a thief,
dropping, as I ran, of Flanders,
Cracow, Vienna and France good coins:
sure I must come to grief.

Yet most were kind. Some offered me
a chair, few blamed the absence of a face.
What saved my happiness, in sum,
was middling courtesy.

Refreshed, I leave a middling tip and rise.
My home is any fragrant history.
When stones have failed, and beams are scarce,
a tent, Vitruvius, must suffice.

THE FOUNTAIN OF TREVI

"Enzo!" "Fabrizio!" "Cafone!"

A brat wades into the basin to retrieve the coins, sopping
shoes, pants and shirt, immemorial and clutchy.

Mothers and fathers and fathers and mothers are bawling
out their slippery kids or wetting them with juicy-
lipped kisses.

And now a fresh damp load of heated tourists. The cameras
salute the statues.

Boys ogle ogled girls. Somebody is selling pictures of exactly
what we're all looking at.

The Fiats and Lambrettas fart into the hubbub, the walls
and shops of the piazza echo the smelly sputter, our
lungs turn black.

Legs dangle as we sit tier on tier; my feet in their sandals
ache like African troopers.

The bearded generation in undershirts and tatters glower or
sleep artistically or munch a crust; the girls look as if
their thoughts if any are fatal.

Suddenly a Midwesterner has offered a horse-and-buggy
man three thousand, who insists like a spinning
record on five, he doesn't work winters, the polyester
wife is miserably embarrassed, they get off, I can't see
who won, the bald head sweats with anger, the horse
clobbers off.

A small policeman launches a monstrous quarrel with five
men, they're having a grand time, like movie Italians,
the kids are yelping to help the quarrel along.

The foreigners are gazing, wonderstruck, at the Fontana,

At the imperious god

The pointed finger

The Triton storming the steeds, the uprushing outrushing
steeds, the imagined clamor of the conch,

Noble the cascade, the leaping stone noble.

Somebody is adding figures on a pad, the day's expenses, and
   picking his nose with the pencil's tiny eraser; his eyes
   bob from the figures to the Figures.

Close to the rim, a foliage of Japanese takes root for a minute
   in "a glory of the West"; their smiles rustle among the
   private syllables.

"Fabrizio, vieni quà, subito!"

Two shrivelled local old ladies have come out for the cool
   air, the horses are so deep in their viscera they will be
   found only at the hour of the supreme recapitulation,
   neighing in stone.

What to do, oh flesh, with the stone's reproof, "Be beautiful,
   you and you, behave with musical rigor, manifest even
   at lunch a palatine demeanor!"

What to do? My feet smell. But we are here, are we not,
   here, not over there, in the suburb, admiring the city
   dump.

And the water is clean, not even the kids throw peels and
   wrappers in it,

And maybe not simply because the little cop is there; who's
   afraid of him anyway? his quarrel swallows him up, you
   could walk away with Mister Neptune.

This congregation I call a beginning, the beginning that has
   been beginning since the beginning,

You marvels, you immortal impossible water and marble
   demand.

[*Cafone*: a boor, a lout. *Vieni quà subito*: Come over here at once. This poem
was written, obviously, in the pre-euro days, and before a glass separation
was installed between basin and spectators.]

BREAKFAST AND JUKEBOX
ON PIAZZA TRASIMENO
(Rome 1960)

Carabinieri on this August morning
when it does me good to see the sun
in its blue dish — although you guard
(keeping an eye on pretty girls and for the rest
making a slouch of it) — although you guard
the Soviet Mission come to sell who knows
what toothsome derricks to Catania
(they hatch their commerce in the sweetest oleandered
loggiad vined and pined palazzo
walls have ever kept from thieves and me),
you will not, will you, keep my Adriana
and myself from dancing one long tango in the street,
to mark, if nothing else, the anniversary of now,
for it was now last year today, and then
last April it was now, and Caesar too
was now, for Caesar did not live in Caesar's past
nor can a clock however sluggish fall behind.

Soldiers! I swear we plot to throw no bomb!
The tango turns us to and fro. They stare at us
my lovely dear, they wonder as we fool about,
if, say, we caught a Russian head amid these pines,
might we not plant a kiss under its cap?
Are they to act in case of sudden bliss?

[Piazza Trasimeno is an inconspicuous little square in a fine residential
area of Rome where the honeymooners had found an affordable *pensione*.
A jukebox was playing in a nearby café.]

CAMERAS

In Piazza Questa or Quella licking my chocolate ice cream
I adorn once more the European tourist scene.

All around the snouts of cameras protrude
To swallow gothic saints, heroes in bronze, and squealing
    brood,

With adventitious me
Included accidentally.

That gives me pause! Say Muse, how many are the silver
    screens,
How many are the album-leaves where, since my teens,

I've done my bit as extra in the crowd
Behind the wives or domes the pictures were about?

In France, Japan, the States, Peru,
Maybe in very Timbuctoo!

I stand, I sit, I gape, I doze,
I eat a grape, I scratch my nose,

Ignored, to make this poem brief, by countless eyes
I can't, alas, advise

That he who slurps the ice cream in the rear is Oscar, me,
    the Only One:
Among the geese an unregarded swan.

[*Questa, quella*: this, that. I have never visited Peru and Timbuctoo, but the
poem doesn't care. As for the fourth stanza, it points, obviously, to an al-
ready distant past in photographic technology.]

ROBBERS

In Naples a gang of experts
cracked our car in the glass cheek
we were lunching standing up a block away
and they knew it

scootered off with our suitcase
leaving a dabble of blood.

The fat women were all over us
we were thumped and yanked with advice good advice
no one had seen a thing.

Now thinking of them standing that suitcase
on a dinky table and counting out my underwear
Adriana's pearls my nice plan for another farce
my blue blazer and the rest, I see these articles
looking around flabbergasted at being pawed
by queer foreigners obviously no friends of the family.

"Where's mom and dad?" cries our property
spitting mad and scared to death.

Lousy gangsters,
are they laughing their heads off round that table?
No, this is business, they're serious,
one of them has a date
to go dancing tonight, Mamma is waiting home
with dinner for the other two,
they're in a hurry
and laughing their heads off.

Listen, children, listen jacket, sweater old friend, suits, shoes,
        pearls,
maybe there's hope: the blood! let's not forget
the good brown blood above the chrome

you couldn't see because you were inside the suitcase.
Hey hey! One of the bastards may be due (pray God)
for grim convulsions witnessed by fainting nurses
maybe he'll die corroded blue and green
from hankering after my underwear.

Yes but where's the satisfaction
where's the bliss
if I don't see it blue and green
with my own two eyes
or read it on page seven under Local News?

If they wind up in a Ferrari
I'm done with this damned galaxy.

MORNING AT CHIAVARI
(Liguria)

A bugling churchbell wakes me,
Proclaiming seven at seven-o-three.
They do it better, if better be better,
In tidy Germany.

TWO VIEWS

1

Place a cottage
in these Dolomites.
In this abominable beauty
place, brother,
a brotherly light.

2

Thrust your elbows, ice,
between these cottages.
Push, colossals,
from too much brother
too much brother.

GENIUS
(Lucerne)

Who has not seen it —
how the water that was strolling
Sunday-like along the river's boulevard,
never quite stopping (as one needn't, you know)
to admire a tree, a gabled house, a Swiss and indolent sheep,
eddying now and then for humor,
twirling a leaf or nudging a sandal that won't sink,
all the while warbling a gurgle nothing like Schubert
yet endearing enough —
how, when banks narrow, it speeds to a crash,
races deep and muscled, the eye cannot follow it,
it whirls, kicks, heaves, swallows, spits
and so resembles genius and is wonderful.

Avoid it, friends.

COL DU GRAND SAINT BERNARD

Glaciers heels up heads down
drivel Rhône or slaver Pô.
From what icy imbeciles
these grandeurs flow!

MORNING IN CHAMONIX

Bread and butter, *un p'tit crème* at the counter,
handshakes for old customers coming in,
the small routine and nicety of gratitude
for my ten francs' worth of business,
then back to the *trottoir* again.

What luck!
Ahead of me steps a girl
born to high heels and brisk decisions.
Her long legs wear a film of hose or pants
(what do I poor bookworm know?) —
wonders of lascivious couture
up which I rise, wishing
Herrick-like I were the tendrils
and the flowers printed there.
Her thighs, praise God, curve just in time
to cup the softest peach of a *derrière*
which rounds again into a waist
two ardent hands could loop a hoop around
with fingers meeting,
drenched by the glissando
of her midnight operatic hair.

Now as she turns a corner
and grim eternity sets in between us
(I'll never, never see her face),
my eyes leap free into the air she left —

More luck!
There hulks and bulks Mont Blanc,
his arms around his hulky-bulky juniors,
and not a cloud this late September
to cap their skulls,
no care but sun and snow and snapshots,

gliders, eagles and *téléfériques*.
What ardors and what squeezings
Went to make such altitudes!
Don't, old worthy lord and mighty tub,
don't go the way the last world empire went
when I return next year to look.

A noise of waking doors and rush of rising shutters
bring Commerce smiling into Chamonix.
Welcome, beaming shops!
Their baubles wink at me
like Antwerp's hookers grinning through their windows.
My purse goes twitching for a trinket.
Paradise, I say,
will keep a corner warm for tinsel.

Nearby, the young green Arve slides under bridges,
all foam and adolescent vehemence,
to wed some aged portly river
in the humdrum plain below;
but there, too high for where my tourist's eye can go,
such luck!
high in cold moss, down breathless rock
it sings itself forever into birth.

There's my hotel, sitting at the curb
like a prim brick governess,
and leashed to her my bulldog of a car,
fed last night, pumped up for Italy,
and all but barking, "Off, man, off, why wait?"

Why wait?
The conifers are humming
slope on slope
a windy need of me.

More into my lungs,
fortunes of morning air!
More, more before I go, and must,
into the hot mouth of the south.

[In spite of its name, a *petit crème* is a large cup of coffee and milk. *Trottoir* means sidewalk. The reference to Herrick is owing especially to "The Vine": "I dreamed this mortal part of mine / Was metamorphosed to a vine, / Which crawling one and every way / Enthralled my dainty Lucia", etc. I enjoyed a view of several prostitutes of Antwerp plying their profession in a house across the narrow street from my oddly named dockside Hotel Antigone. The Arve flows, I believe, into the Rhône at Geneva.]

COLONEL PLUCHOT CHATS WITH MADAME DUCHESNE

Strolling on the beach and perking up my tan
(Scene: the Plage Municipale in Cannes)

I come across — dear me — what *is* her name again? —
Good! just in time! — "Ah, madame Duchesne!" —

(They own the "Arts de Chine" bazar on rue Pasteur).
The lady rises briskly from her lounging chair —

"Colonel Pluchot! How *do* you do!"
We shake hands — her naked bosom in full view —

"I ran into *Madame* Pluchot at Rohr's last Saturday!"
Good God, a girl of twenty would be proud of that display.

I smile. "Your husband's on the road, madame?"
          "To be sure —
He lands today, poor dear, in Singapore" —

(The place, I take it, for the better grade
Of tourist fakes in plastic, ivory or jade).

"To the Alps again in August, sir?"
"We might — " "Such luck! Alas, *we* cannot stir."

"Enjoy the beach, madame, the hordes are coming soon!"
Two pink nuggets nuzzled each one on its moon....

Consider though: to veer my gaze above her bust
Would show embarrassing embarrassment, so gaze I must.

"D'you think, madame, the tale about our mayor's true?"
"I don't! Jesus Christ was slandered too.

Monsieur Mouillot has always been most kind to *us*,
So why — " "Well, they do say — " "Why all the fuss?"

And so we talk — a bit of this, a bit of that —
We own a spaniel, they a cat —

"Goodness! Two Rolls-Royces stolen from a sheik!"
"Eight are left, madame, the *Nice-Matin* reported without
        tongue in cheek."

These pleasantries, I've found,
Do help to make the world go round.

Another handshake, and so ends this episode
Of no especial note.

Now, however, let your fancy lift and set
Our chit-chat fifty paces off, on the Croisette,

Or on the rue d'Antibes chez Rohr —
Same words, same bosom — fifty feet away, no more! —

The fancy tries, it yanks, it pulls, the scene won't go;
Madame Duchesne would die, yes die! before she'd show,

Smack on the street, without distress,
Her ruddy teats in undisguised undress.

Bizarre! Something is here, I do believe, philosophers could
 sift.
Me? An old retired soldier? I'll take a dip, cool off, and drift.

[Rohr is a good pastry-shop in the rue d'Antibes, which runs in elegant
parallel to the seaside promenade, the Croisette. The financial scandals con-
cerning the mayor, monsieur Mouillot, took place in 1996, and eventually
landed him in jail. In the same year the Rolls-Royces were stolen.]

A CHILD AT THE SEASIDE

Her mother prods her
into a tiny frizzling wave.
She lunges, laughs, waddles back, cries, attacks again, babbles
 at the spray.
The Mediterranean kittens with her shins and submits.
Centuries old, the mother, smiling, playing, prattling and
 watching,
folds the child into the world.

Somewhere, the fates are teaching
a newborn ant how to carry a speck.

Lying in the sand, repeated and repeating,
I blink for the hundred forty millionth time.

ON THE BEACH

A moppet asks:
"How many sand is there in the whole wide world?"
I answer:
"Fifty-seven dillion grillion killion."

Because I do not care.
It's only when I think of us and us and us:
Then I begin to sweat.
Back, child, back to sand,
Pick up your shovel and play.

LOW TIDE AND HIGH TIDE
IN NORMANDY
(Houlgate)

For our hosts Janine and Claude Lasry

The sea, as if absconded to another planet,
leaving dabs of mementoes: zebra-ridges of sand
that tweak the arches of bare feet,
crunched shells streaked out like Milky Ways,
sleepy streamlets, pools and puddles
where, musing poems, back and forth I rhyme my toes.

Overhead the dreadnought clouds
ship in on winds not even young Demosthenes
could have orated down
had he at Houlgate put its pebbles in his mouth.
Tents and beach-chairs
clap their fabric as if applauding their tormentor,
while the kites jig-jag faking indignation

or haul across the sand
bottoms of red-cheeked boys bleating with happiness.

Unflapped (for wind is to Houlgate what roaring is to lions)
more tots carve out their holes and build their castles,
winsome clones of me when imp of nine or ten
I dabbled in the sands of cozy Flanders
(Flanders, where pious to the preaching wind
the poplars bend in unison toward the East),
and for a moment as I watch the children
and the thread to mother which they cannot see,
my own, my caring dear, returns, and waves me back to her.

Unbuffeted, a school of horses, svelte, sedate
(I wish they could rejoice in their paraded dignity)
carry young jockeys straight across the rim,
their little bodies nodding, nodding as they ride.

Miles off (it seems) I gather human punctuations —
clam-diggers they are whose bellies and souls
harmonize in adoration of nature:
"joindre l'utile à l'agréable", they might call it,
bent over shovels and buckets and picking up
between drafts of sublimity a juicy meal.

And who sits there? She's the recording angel:
a cloaked and scarved and hatted mass at an easel
doing Boudin's work behind a wind-screen,
inspecting, but inspected: she sees a world,
I see the world she sees and her who sees it.
Fifty steps and I'd be sucked into her canvas;
instead it's I who throw my net and haul her in,
edible for this my poem.

No windscreen for me.
Impudent to the gale,
I fight with both my hands for my cap's loyalty.

Doff it to me! Doff it to me! whizzes the wind.
But I won't, and with gleeful tears in my eyes,
swallowing balloons of air,
and ramming onward,
I stagger to the street at last,

Where the wind gives up without a fight.
Like a pricked balloon
pop, the roaring brute has swooned.
Normalcy takes me aback:
the chingaling of a bicycle meeting a pedestrian,
the neighborly slam of a gate,
and, up the stairs,
three friendly voices and a table neatly set.

"Vous apportez le pain, Jocelyne?"

Knife aloft,
fine sauce of chat,
fork into gullet,
attentive, held, yet yawning,
I yearn toward my pillow.

Easing into sleep, I know that when I wake
a swollen sea, full of itself,
bullying the doorsill of the seedy old casino,
will taunt me that I merely dreamed of sand.
"Sand almost till England?
Sand, the bib Houlgate never takes off?
Fathoms deep, odd friend,
all a-gurgle, look for beach!
There crabs will testify the kites were in your head,
the castles sandy ghosts
arrived by chance from windy Flanders."
And walking out this afternoon
I'll find Madame Boudin squat on the "promenade"
(an asphalt strip Deauville would laugh at)

toiling at the sea into whose foam, bending her bulk,
she could dip her brush —
those ardent waters which, like all perfections,
low tide and high,
will not let another in, saying: choose!

[Houlgate (pronounced Ool-gatt in French) is an unassuming seaside resort
between fashionable Deauville and Proust's still elegant Cabourg. Eugène-
Louis Boudin (1824-1898) painted his lovely beach scenes in the days when
fully dressed ladies and gentlemen sat on the sand in stiff chairs. The two
French phrases: "Joining the useful to the pleasant" and "You're bringing the
bread, Jocelyne?"]

DAWN AT THE MANOR
OF CERISY-LA-SALLE

A cow's pensive baritone
accompanies my slow waking,
and of regardless birds the merry fife.
Near my bed (a baron's ease) the window gestures
 toward summer and a doom of wasps;
they drone their testament in unison,
one by one they die, sunlit, upon the sill.

Attentive for the breakfast gong
a rugged hand will soon be swinging,
I loll to the parish church whose bell
the fickle ocean wind now swells,
and now heretically numbs.

A fuss of gravel underneath announces man,
paths primly raked, prudent hedges,
and pots that cinch their plants,

as if those heathen flowers peppering
the manor's meadows to the end of view
threatened jacobin disorders to the mind.

A whisper comes to me:
Here, now, just now,
all contraries are innocent...

Dreaming myself awake,
I yawn mild thoughts into my pillow.
My past becomes the muddy spaniel
shaking his hide out of a brook
as we strolled amused among the hedgerows.
And my future,
to sit in silence on a bench of stone
friendly to decades of scholars,
and watch, forgotten of my griefs,
a slow beatitude of cows munching Normandy away,
their tails beating time and, now and then,
like lazy constables,
thwacking a malicious fly.

[Every summer a learned foundation offers a series of conferences on a variety of topics at the manor-house of Cerisy-la-Salle, in Normandy, near the cathedral town of Coutances. Distinguished scholars lead and speak, paying guests listen, discuss, or idle time away along the meadows, the pond, the gardens, the farm.]

ONE MINUTE BEFORE NOON

One minute before noon.
Two cows are galloping in Normandy.
God dozes. Humble flowers powder the grass.

A caterpillar millimetres on a stone.
The road, fondling a tractor in its lap,
Slips under a hill. A rooster soloes.
A wall loses a sliver. Nothing dies.

Noon noon, ding the churchbells, noon noon.

God's awake!

A wasp and I exchange an ugly look.

[In its first printed version, I marked this poem "Cerisy-la-Salle, July 27, 1978". It was begotten by the sight, new for a city-dweller like myself, of two fully grown cows dashing across the meadow that stretches far off from the manor.]

THE RADICAL VISITS LA BAULE

Let her enjoy her crème de menthe while she has it,
  The rich old biddy
  On the terrace at La Baule.

Varnished, niftied, poodled, girdled, jewelled —
  Jeezes it's like seeing
  A tombstone crack a smile.

Make no mistake, her cops'll bite your head off
  If they catch you tying your shoelace
  Against her U.S. Cadillac.

When she was born and belched her first squawk
  They underpaid five females to go
  Goo goo goo and look like they meant it.

And when she buys a hanky she gets chauffeured to it
  And a six-foot goon
  Trundles it out for her.
Go on, drink up, but wait, we'll blast the opal off your finger,
  We'll make you eat your Louis Fifteen,
  You'll scrub latrines down on your knees,

And never mind who'll wear the bloody opal next.

[La Baule, seaside resort in Brittany, where the sight of a wealthy matron at
a nearby table inspired this dramatic monologue in the days when Commu-
nism was still an admired or a dreaded force.]

THE CLOCK IN THE
AMSTERDAM FLEA MARKET

(I'll call it he, may I?) He'd come on wicked times
and hadn't tried to set them right since ages long,
he couldn't tick, he'd lost his chimes,
the key was gone, and now they'd made him sit among
disgraceful skirts, cracked tables and a perishing rug —
so bad four Dutchmen grinned when I
(dumb tourist) asked to pick him up,
and "Will it work?" I risked, and "Yes I'll try."

He wasn't what the Spanish Court would offer Louis
nor made to be a bribe sent to a greedy Pope;
no dolphin on his pate, no naiad on his knee,
no amethyst or silver Faith and Hope;
plain wood he stood, plain honest face,
Dutch homely square
and solid Calvinistic grace,
one flower carved into his chest with modest care

to show he'd lived with delft and lace
before his reprobation to a slum.

I gave my seven guilders, found somewhere a key,
affixed a vagrant pendulum,
turned nuts and screws, and set him free.
With feeble health and anxious grain he sat
and pressed a cushion in my car
to make and to survive the journey to my flat.
The city is not plush. A street gave us a jar,
then twenty more, with cobblestones and tramway rails
and turns to take and brakes to squeeze and stops to make.
They poked him into clucks and wails
and whirrs, a wooden ache,
a knocking rib, slim gongs
of fright and twangs of trouble,
in short, a hospital of wrongs.
But when at home I set him upright in his rubble
and looking like a magistrate
whose mien ascribes his belch to creaking furniture,
I swore, come landlord, wife or maid,
come blossom or come burr,
to hoist him up on any shelf I'd ever own,
well-dusted, wound and decently displayed.

I've kept my word. The years dropped in, went home.
The hours migrated chime by chime.
Sometimes I heard, but mostly not, his mild trustworthy sign
the planks are rotting under me and like a wrinkled child
I must fall down, there is no hold.
He's grown a touch more grim of late;
his voice a pulpit's weight,
hard not to note and mind.
No matter. I prefer the sentence tolled
his way: ticking Death almost benign:
domesticated Fate.

[I picked up this clock in 1960 or 1961, the year I lectured on American poetry at the University of Amsterdam, and I must have written a first draft of the poem soon after the little event.]

FLIGHT 065

Humbly seated in tourist class,
I muse on those who invent these roarers,
The pilots, the mechanics, and the rest
Who turn the sky into almost a sofa.
But wait — the reliables are everywhere :
"A job well done" is no rarity —
The water in our faucets clean to drink,
The nuclear power works we don't panic at,
Holes in the asphalt decently filled,
Violins quite as good as Guarnieris....
I tell myself, as the Boeing tucks me in,
All is not fraud, all is not carnage !
Now and then one dares to breathe.

FROM CHIHUAHUA TO THE BORDER

What they do out there, the mountains, is stand
stark useless; bleach (but why?) glued to the sun;
not one green hair grows on these rumps nor is heard
one woosh of a wing or grumble of a throat.
The road's a slap at them they don't know how to feel.
They wall me up (driving north) on either side
of one brown prostrate earth,
I give them blank for blank,
until oh God who was it winked at them?

You, you, behind my yawn, you femurs,
ribcage, mandibles, sworn friends to me, you
plotting with foreigners, assassins in my house!

No, we love you, sing the bones, drive on, drive on.

CAMP GORDON
(Georgia 1953)

In recollection of the time in the hot hospital
down in Georgia in the United States
with pneumonia caught inhaling murder
and drilling with the jolly men
God had blasphemed against the earth:

they paid him back the same.

First sick call
where they believed my fever
and authenticated the fainting I had done
with such dark paradise of soul that day
marching to the tom-tom of the head-hunter sun.

Second the trouble with the human item at the desk
who asked me "your religion, bud?"
to fill a certain blank in case of death
and shivering I said None, before God none,
none by God, goddamit none
until they found a bed for me in a ward
full of his youngsters, black and pink,
the ones He jettisoned all over earth:

they paid him back the same.

That was a sweet pneumonia
although my orders were I must survive.
I did not eat the pills,
I rubbed thermometers, I groaned,
but slowly I recovered, I began to hear
the seven radios of the ward:
Love howling to the plik-plik of guitars,
trombones bleating, drumbeats raging,
preachers, sellers, quizzers, chatters,
trumpets cymbals saxophones: a soup of noise
their God had slopped down on the earth:

they paid him back the same.

At night I went in slippers and pajamas
to a patch of something almost grass
behind a door I shut.
I walked criss-cross and in a circle,
hearing honest insects chirp,
and while I walked, I sang against my time
cantatas I invented from remembered scraps.
I sang like a demented naked man
the cops haul off the street
while all the damsels laugh to see his human skin,
then I returned to bed, the lights went out,
and no one knew
I had then overthrown our consecrated State,
the duly constituted government of man.
Now I slept, awaiting orders,
between a cussing private and a beery corporal
God has fumed against the earth:

they pay him back the same.

RAINY SEASON IN BARRACKS
(Camp Fuji 1954)

On Sunday all the rain fell down.
We cursed. Then Fuji disappeared,
Although he stood so close, blue days
We soldiers mucked his gown.

The roofs were drumming, midnight fell at six,
The grass swam in a soup of mud.
We gargled air and used wet hands
To squeeze the water from our cheeks.

On Sunday Shunkwan smiled and gave a wink.
He said, "Suns too must sleep." One could not walk,
One could not pay nephews a call,
But one could think.

We cursed some more, next boredom made us ill,
But then we drank such Yankee gin
That fists began to jazz. And Shunkwan said,
"Each man improves according to his skill."

IN A DEMOCRACY

housewife, brat, poet, welder, banker,
everybody has a Fate
a huge contraption of grief and bliss
protruding, insisting
on picky attention from professionals:
millions of Fates in tandem or criss-cross
each granted its high decibels
in the boom-boom-boom of history.

O dust.

EMPTY HOUSE

In the middle of my house
a clock strikes one
(it does?)
to no one.

Vibrations lunge
(do they?)
at chairs and sleeping
canapés.

Why does the world
bother to be
without me?

At two,
a shift in dust
proves a vibration
was, and must.

Or did dust shift
to rendez-vous
with my two eyes
at two?

Why does the world
bother to be
without me?

Stars drumming
ten billion years,
and not even
a pair of ears?

[A *canapé* is a sofa.]

THE ASTRONAUT ATE A PIECE
OF CONSECRATED BREAD
ON THE MOON (1969)

The Reverend blessed a loaf of bread,
Aldrin flew it to the moon,
To prove man is and shall remain
Half sage, two-thirds buffoon.

LET US DREAM (1)

Time lays out good times like beads upon a string,
A kiss, a touch of praise, a music, spring.
Paradise be simultaneous everything,
Eternity obviate remembering.

LET US DREAM (2)

If there is heaven it must be simplicity
where nuns will dancing be
with heavy-hearted lads and girls
dance and dance with puzzled chemists
and dancing kiss
the desperado atheists.

Where every cross becomes a parallel
timelessness may make us well,
and prove
profundity a spoof,
problems mistaken, and complication hell.

Two: Busy Eros

The poems in this "chapter" are all from decades of my life when the god of love was busiest needling me, albeit the aging reviser in me has often been unfaithful to the young fellow's words of bliss and grief. The arrangement I have made here, roughly from happy expectation and fulfillment to disappointed snarl (must poetry be "nice"?) is therefore artificial — made to look deceitfully as though a single story curved from beginning to end.

FEVER

The man you choose to love
should disbelieve in rain
praise dogs for singing
tickle generals under the stubbled chin
and never die.

I myself am nearly come to this,
because you threw me, absent-mindedly,
one entire courteous word.

FALLING

Love is swift
inevitability.
Drop an acorn
down that tree.
If there's no choice
but earth for it,
that acorn's me.

PLENITUDE

I sing under my beard
a basso folderol of note.
The cat cancels no promenade,
I jostle neither sun nor mote.

I sing the crazy mood a leper has
come back new-fangled to the street.

The windows do not rattle
and parallels don't meet.

Suspicious by my door,
the reassured gendarme
returns his pistol to his belt,
reports the situation calm.

YOUNG PAN
HAULS METHODISTS AWAY

It's sienna all the way,
It's lady-slippers, grass deliriums.
No bookish God is peeping
With a scimitar inside his fist
These hours droll with liberty.
So let's abuse a clover bed
And pull the wind about us
Like a coverlet. Oh splendid news!
One hundred horses drive the sun,
Young Pan hauls Methodists away,
And flights of nuns are caught
In zigzags of vociferous bees....

SONG

Today April today
the new grass jungles
and green birds play.

A high-strung
wind conceals
his sentimental lung,

grumbles
where a bud babies
and fumbles,

and terrifies
a newborn moth
with jests of ice,

while high
the sun on ladder clouds
repaints the sky.

This week April this week
Eros flies in,
smiling in Greek.

My young eye swarms
where ready girls
bare dangerous arms.

Before tongues dare,
decisions dart,
we flirt mid-air.

We have no name,
we never met,
but all the same

we prophecy
the kiss the quarrel
the promise the sigh,

and long "shall we?"
as flower bends
to flowering bee,

as moon slips out
her grasping
corpulent cloud,

and ocean lifts
his waves where she
soever drifts.

THE TWENTY-SIXTH OF APRIL

The twenty-sixth of April warm needles
Are reported in the air.
Our sun blooms elegant. In areas of noon
Young suicidal men who dwelled all winter
On a ragged incunabulum
Have come within the beckon of a dancing foot.
Consider, Liz! an inkling of the wind
Speeds all the leaflets to each others' arms,
A touch of Spring suasion
Puts the candles to their prayers
In the first-come chestnut tree,
Azaleas set themselves on fire,
And the cocked eye of the sun
Stirs every crocus from his pillow.
Oh Liz, why should two lovers shuffle
Who could, if they'd but half agree,
Ignite the scene perennially?

FOUR HANDS WHISPER AND DO

Elizabeth for long.
That is official
and in company:
a bow to the throng,
handsome gentility.

Liz for short.
The sound's like the quip
of a bee snatching
pollen for sport,
and buzzing her wing.

But *Lisa* is the time
four hands whisper and do
in two bodies' nooks
like children at their little crimes
when nobody looks.

A BANKER SOBBING ON HIS TYPIST

Say, what will I see, Elizabeth —
A pink-haired dogwood in December —
A banker sobbing on his typist
For the sin of being rich —
Spider with his rueful legs giving
Flies their liberty — hare calling
Her hunter — ribald saint — Buddha in a pet?
Or, love, continuance of love,
Decanted once with such a dipping
Of the heart, I thought I'd drunk of it,
Poor me, a minor immortality?

[The three Elizabeth poems of this "chapter", and several others in which she is not named, go back to the years 1948-1951 when I was studying and teaching at the Ohio State University. I have forgotten nothing except the (married) girl's last name!]

MY LOVE ANSWERS MY LOVE

My love answers my love;
    into lips lips sink
and one same milk,
    each other, drink.

What are to us
    chaos and flood?
Our love is dumb
    to other blood.

The cannon's concussion
    finds us asleep
like harvesters blithe
    after the reap.

No broadcast tells the world
    its chemistry is changed
or by two dots of love
    republics rearranged.

Month buries our day,
    year raises our stone;
the winds come rubbing,
    rubbing us unknown.

AFTER HERRICK

swiftly the apple born
the apple praised
the apple rotten.

swiftly we two
we too
forgotten.

THE GARDEN

I place you in a garden
a garden twenty times
as fair as paradise,
perfumed with flowers
that shrug at seasons,
a garden where a toadstool would get lost
if a toadstool could be found
disgracing in my garden
twenty times
as good
as paradise.

And over it an orange sun
contracted for eleven in the morning
in incessant May,
a cloud or two
for humor and trees
trees making a great windy rush
to stay precisely where they are,
near you that is,
spying out of every green and rascal leaf.

And round about
I stick a wide and nasty wall
made of the foulest foul brown stone,
besides electric wires, spikes,
and here and there a hungry dog.
As I can't fly
I add a stingy gate
locked by a ton of steel
to which the only key sits in my pocket.
The gate is smart and understands
I am here king and janitor.

The rest? I'll eat my tongue.
When it is I come,
and how it is you greet me,
the weight and contour of our dialogues,
the kiss that interferes
with topics of importance,
the bodies in their moist entanglements,
you know, I know,
we spread no gospels —
although that daisy
standing by our keels its yellow eye wide open
that daisy I suspect
is learning dimly in its roots
there's more to Nature
than the bureaucrats of pollen
and the sniff of lowly snouts.

[Forty or fifty years before 2014, when the first draft of this poem was com-
posed, one could, I believe, sing of a man imprisoning a woman (metaphor-
ically, to be sure) without so much as an afterthought.]

NO MORE POEMS

The days I wept Ah woe is me
I sobbed a bucket-full of poetry.
But now, unlocked her door,
Drop, dumb pen, drop to the floor.

THE ROMANTIC MATERIALIST

I gave my love long kisses thigh to thigh
   December night, the solstice of our love,
   ascending toward the Christmas of the seed
   and feeding our poor universe with yet
another bone devoted to a bone.

For all we knew that love is fiber, tissue,
   cell leaping with intelligence of cell,
   we ranted "soul" we raved "enchantment":
   two compounds ionized into romance:
vain rebellion, smiled the atoms in their whirl.

THE JAIL

Sentenced to
the universe of me
let lips, let arms debar
that worse jail, liberty.

You'd breathe
with a constricted chest
independent
on an Everest.

Since Adam
poor man went and sinned
kindly walls stand
to the cruel wind.

THE JOURNEY

For three days, good-bye,
and in that thimble of time
oceans of apprehension lie.

LOVER'S MAXIM

The wounds of love bleed boiling red.
Prudence, dear, is colored dead.

UNSAFE I REPLY

Lovers, like emperors
    of crumbling Rome,
sway proudest and strongest
    the first day of throne.

Their stride and their spring
    are such as gave men
the mystic notion
    of life without sin.

Limber with worship,
  calm after lust,
they admire a crumb
  and smile at dust.

What follows we know:
  spies in the cellars,
rumors, snide remarks
  of fortune-tellers,

an old, lyrical rose
  left in a gully,
tantrums of fears,
  and then the last folly,

not to depart
  but sullenly sit
clutching crowns and rings
  that no longer fit.

To this, says divination,
  we must come as well:
love is a nomad,
  duration his hell.

He comes like a storm
  uprooting the trees;
he goes like the hem
  of a tattered breeze.

Unsafe I reply:
  hide lowly with me,
huddle in cellars
  beneath history,

and plot to continue
  passionate fools
obscure to the notice
  of maxims and rules.

THWARTED LOVER

Some death fetches like a brisk police
that collars innocents at drink
or lovers at their kiss.

But cowards run
to their own tomb
(a funeral of one
into her own cocoon).

As if they couldn't wait,
they dig a solid hole
and sneak under a cross
to smother their own soul.

You, girl, are one of such.
I pleaded break
your dolls and idols, burn
a city for our sake,

cross husband, mother, God,
fool inconvenient laws,
love passion and rank honesty
and loathe peculiarly remorse.

But you, not answering,
resigned me with a sigh,
like an incurable
unwilling not to die.

REPINE, REPINE

If it is ill to be an underground
And dry he-was, it is much worse to roam
By arctic cliffs where seals are shivering
And sunlight rarely interlopes, and know
You dance meantime inside the circle
Of heartwhole fat peonies. Death is not cruel
Since we're all lost; it's caste I hate: to be
The varlet while a princess plies her minuet.

WOUNDED PHILOSOPHER

They note that I am glum. They ask me why.
"Crime is not crime. God is a lie.

The sun will burst. Earth is a sty.
Nor saved nor damned I die.

Are these not cause enough?" They nod: "The man is deep."
Nitwits! My mistress left. I weep.

Explanatory note

Shall ontologic pain be more
Than, say, my thumb caught in the door?

THE EGG THE MOTHER THREW

The egg the Mother threw
that sprouted the first man,
Egypt, Ur and Babylon,
has hatched (don't giggle) me and you,

58

to raise this bedtime doubt:
was all that fuss
to culminate in naked us,
are we what bibles sing about?

Go wash, and pin your hair,
and let us, while I knot my tie,
submit that in our Mother's eye
we are, like Christ and bread, just there.

OTHERS ARE MORE IMPORTANT

Let me wholly put my mind
To Caracalla's frightened Rome,
To Albigensians burning
Pimple, hair and toe,
To sick and starving, maimed and blind.

Humane lament will tell
My own, perhaps, to blush,
For though I sulk and bite my lip,
My grief lies not on earth's
Noteworthy parallel.

[When the first version of this poem was printed in 1960, the fifth line read: "To Europe rationing a rind," proof that it was written close, or fairly close, to the end of World War II. In 1981, I substituted "Asia" for "Europe". But in the 21st century even "Asia" — fortunately — no longer fits (by and large), hence the line has been generalized. The reader must decide whether the inversion "lies not" in the penultimate line is a weak archaism or, for once, an admissible move.]

FOUL MOOD

The wise and the good will not fool me,
mine's the tough language of sense:
not *this* for books and dress
and *that* for muddy Tuesdays.

Oh yes, I've heard of selfless love,
immortality, free choice, our duties,
and the unique consciousness of man;
who hasn't heard rave the wise and the good?

Come, woman, undress, your husband's away,
your children snore, time ticks and is gone.
Root your fingers in the soil I am.
I shall leave you at the first noble word.

BRUTE ENGLISH

I am weary of the lyric grape
(nature, take me dumb)
of "mist lifting out of brown cattails",
of winds' "contorted strength",
of "pink rice grains" for stars,
of "undinal vast belly"
of the sea, and all such annotations.
The bees and leaves have been exalted,
nature, take me dumb.

I am weary of the topic love
(woman, love me dumb)
of "willow eyelids", of "intense fragility",
twin breasts "cooing like doves under the eaves",
of thighs "like papal marble", of moans

for love's regrettable delinquencies.
Woman, love me dumb:
though eyes may be "deeper than roses",
brute English is my tongue.

[Decades after composition, I have forgotten the source of the lyric images
I quote, but I do remember that they are genuine quotations, and all from a
twentieth-century poet, man or woman.]

SULLEN MYRMIDONS (1)

Sullen Myrmidons poison the weeds
Lest an enemy survive.

In a ruin two lovers huddle.
A booted lout guffaws.

In his low brain one atom shifts.
We must love on.

SULLEN MYRMIDONS (2)

Sullen Myrmidons poison the weeds
Lest an enemy survive.

In a ruin two lovers huddle.
A booted lout guffaws.

In his low brain no atom shifts.
We must love on.

[The substitution of a single tiny word for another makes for a huge differ-
ence in meaning, yet aesthetically none.]

Three: Names

Here I have used as my ordering principle names of important personages, real or fictive, summoned in the roughly chronological sequence of their existence or creation.

"THE GREAT LACK OF OUR TIME
IS THAT WE HAVE
NO COMMANDING MYTH
TO WHICH WE CAN GIVE ALLEGIANCE"

That Eve and Snake made brisk alliance
Was honest postlapsarian science,
Saying 'Kindly do not label
The grand thing a fable.'

Nor was it mythically meant
That Atlas' daughters wafted to the firmament,
Though in truth's late avatar
There's little stuff but helium in a star.

And Christ was fact, and so was Osiris.
Myth *was*, but never *is*.
Time was when gods were killed to foil starvation.
We have irrigation.

Are they too bleak, the bonds of nitrogen?
Our sons will sigh for time was when
An atom hung from every eave,
And men were happy, for they could believe.

[The quotation which furnishes the title of my poem comes from an essay by Babette Deutsch, but the thought is a commonplace of our times. Whatever may be the official pronunciation, here Osiris is to be spoken as a dactyl: OZZ-i-ris.]

IMMORTALITY

Who's Diphilos? His works are lost.
He was a poet time was when,
Won some prizes, made a dent
In Greece among the better men,

And got tossed out one time
Because he wrote a stupid comedy.
Ten scholars now remember him.
That too is immortality.

[Here again, the name should be pronounced as a dactyl: DIPH-i-los.]

EMPEDOCLES

Empedocles stood on the crater's rim
And looked inside at boil and muck and din.

In his right hand (or left) he held a cup
Full of the best Falernian sold in a Sicilian pub.

He didn't drink but poured it slowly down instead
Into the crater's horrid heaving bed.

Not since the universe began (that's long ago)
Had wine met with the pitch it met below;

And yet, as wise Empedocles could see,
Nor pitch nor wine consulted Greek philosophy

To do at once — I don't know what, I wasn't there —
Whatever Nature's law expected of the pair.

Instead, our man kept diddling "Should I jump or not?"
And stood there daylong tying & untying that mental knot

Before he cried, "Infernal Powers! I come! Spread wide your
    gates!"
Human is the stuff that hesitates.

WAR DITTY (1)

Alcaeus, Horace and Anacreon,
Good cowards all (though brave in song),
I too grew nervous, dropped my gun,
And voted medals for the strong.

I favored too the striking of a kiss
Above the tantrums of a bomb;
I did my duty to my private bliss,
Alcaeus, Horace and Anacreon.

[These lyric poets, like Archilochus before them, all fled in battle: the first
from the Athenians in their war against his native Lesbos in the sixth cen-
tury B.C., the second at the Battle of Philippi in 42 B.C. in which Antony
and Octavian defeated and killed Brutus and Cassius, and the third — again
in the sixth century B.C. — from Cyrus the Great, founder of the Persian
empire. The first person of the poem is of course simply "a speaker".]

THE LIFE AND DEATH OF HANNIBAL

Oh Hannibal, I wish that I could ride an elephant,
and wipe my boot against an Alp.
I wish that I could suffer like a helmet
and lick sorbets while temples fall.

But you're the man, hard Hannibal, who plunges
out of camps of edelweiss. You toss
the matrons of Campania to your chocolate boys.
Moustache erect, you call for poison, and you quaff.

TO OVID, FROM ARMY BARRACKS

Rome drove you from the middle of a repartee
Far from the Forum and the late levées,
Beyond the unctuous slaves, the wicked plays,
To growl, they hoped, with Scythians of the gross black sea.
There you continued laughably to pare your nails
(While your grim neighbors tore at meat with theirs);
You cited Virgil, kept some small parterres,
Slept early. Hags in the woods boiled skins and scales.
Clutching your mother past, you took your pen again,
And weeping toward Caesar on his hill,
The song was Rome, the art was Roman still:
The syllables kept order in their pain.

[The barracks of the title are those I lived in either at Camp Gordon in
Georgia or at Camp Fuji in Japan (see "Rainy season in barracks") during
my military service from 1953 to 1955. A *levée* is a "morning assembly held
by a prince or person of distinction". A *parterre* is a well-groomed level part
of a garden.]

HOLY BOOKS

Christ is bad and Moses worse;
Montaigne fills my mental purse.

(Re the Number 3 Strong Cheese —
Bullets and bombs! I'll hold my peace).

ON RE-READING
THE NEW TESTAMENT

How could grown-up men,
More gifted thousandfold than I,
Upon this hocus-pocus
Cathedrals edify?

Yet how dry to think like me,
Hard, straight and pointed as a nail.
Give Milton his angels
Lest his iambs fail!

THE VISION OF JESUS OF NAZARETH
CONCERNING
JOHANN SEBASTIAN BACH

Why do I carry this splintered wood upon my back,
Why do I suffer the children to grin thornily,
Why do I grant my nakedness to be seen
Crucified under my willing Father
(Father I dread the hurt for all my soul's solidity),

And why am I who am the Son of God
Dirtily dying by hammer and by spike?
I am in canon with my future. I cry
But dwell upon my echo. I drag the cross,
But far, far off, divine, the choir sings.

[The art inspired by religions (all religions) is perhaps the only type of *un-alloyed* good that comes of them.]

THE ATHEIST

My mind dwelling perfectly on death's incommodation
cries "Away with soothing literature
and lofty wisdom!" — that famous Roman
calm at his blather before they broke him on the rack....

The night I opened Hell and saw Ugolino set
his teeth into Ruggieri's hair, I turned my head away,
but slow enough I caught a muddy swinish grin,
and then the teeth hit bone and I was forced to look.

His hair bleeding (and Ugolino's upper lip
was pushed against the nose from biting) Ruggieri grinned,
Ruggieri said: "Yet I am I", and I crouched stunned.
There is no cruelty to match no God at all.

Me for the rectangular bed, bad earth
my blanket, bone and beneath ache,
not even wishing someone drilled a hole and thrust
a tube to periscope some sky to me.

Eternal blank, worse than any pain.

[That famous Roman: Boethius, writing *The Consolation of Philosophy* before dying in prison in the year 524. The Hell of the poem is of course Dante's, Canti XXXII and XXXIII.]

A DITTY SUNG BY A CHOIR
OF AGING POETS
(AMONG THEM SOPHOCLES,
SHAKESPEARE AND GOETHE)

Young, cocksure and immune,
We sang fortissimo of ghastliness and doom.
Now, goose-pimpled near our icy tomb,
Of happy endings we prefer to croon.

[I had in mind *Oedipus at Colonus*, *The Tempest* and the finale of *Faust Part II*. The old don't like to visit graveyards.]

IAGO

Give him his due:
when Iago finished
his act,

Iago shut his mouth.
There was no chatter
in the man,

no urge
to start careers
after extinction.

THE INFANTRYMAN AND BAUDELAIRE

Poor Charles he took his sins so seriously;
each time he bought a drink Man fell again;
he suffered himalayas; demons pinched him:
symbols oh yes, but still they smelled,

they had the good authentic gothic air
of meaning blood and dealing hell
and swatting men between a woman's breasts.
Maybe he'd loved his chère maman too much,

poor Charles, but come, it must have been quite nice
to feel that Lucifer himself broke through
Voltaire to damn him in particular
for lapping at a Caribbean wench;

it must have been a treat to face a God
you could shock half to death by showing him
where two of his bare daughters fooled against
the code, "Their ghastly cult unhinged the sun."

I envy you. I murdered women, children, men
last war by soaking them in flames,
the rest are weeping starved and sick,
and what I say is "yeah, too bad" and look about,

afraid I've overdone the fancy rhetoric.

THE CONCEPTIONS OF THE INTELLECT

Fool of a Freudian,
what if God has legislated
we shall light upon Him (glory glory!)
through the bearded figure of a mortal dad?

Fool of a Christian
to believe it might be so.

Three o'clock: on the lake
the sun places a flock of suns,
which a smiling wind erases
at three o'clock and three.

WAR DITTY (2)

Wilfred Owen died in the World War
The darling of his rifle corps.

He volunteered, the way a great man ought,
And can't complain that he was shot.

I squinted, said I could not see;
The doctors scowled, got rid of me.

Unpatriotic to the core,
I plan to live to ninety-four.

[This poem is imaginary bravado, since I spent two years in the American army. In an earlier version (called "Ditty on the Brave Man's Lot"), the last two lines read:

> I hate my land, hate mankind more,
> And plan to live to ninety-four.

Too strong, and a far stretch beyond the truth, yet better, I think, as poetry. An interesting dilemma. Both versions have what scholars call "authority".]

ROBERT FROST:
"I'D AS SOON MAKE LOVE IN LOVER'S LANE AS WRITE FOR LITTLE MAGAZINES"

If, dear sir, I hadn't saved my dollars in a roll
To pay a landlord's toll
For neatly swept suburban flat,
And if, distinguished sir, I didn't own a welcome mat
And two Kandinskys (copies to be sure),
A living-room with Danish furniture,
And bonbons for my honey in a silver dish,
A kitchen furthermore with a sweet niche
Where two can breakfast on Bavarian ware
(If it so happens two are there),
And had I not a confidential bed
With lissom sheets and quilted coverlet,
A rug for pretty naked feet,
A burner with ecstatic heat,
And drapes to baffle streetlights when they come
(The boors) to see is anybody home —
If, in short, I couldn't love my mistress
Respectably upon a mattress,
I'd do it (braving frost) cramped in Lover's Lane
Between the dashboard and the window-pane,
And there I might beget, surprise!
A hero fit, like you, for Paradise.

[There was a time when literary quarterlies and the like were called "little magazines".]

MEDITATION ON WALLACE STEVENS'
"THE IMPERFECT IS OUR PARADISE"

I too, undoubtedly, I too
I should have ventured to conceive this world
as turquoise, aware but softly
of the streak that marred its blue primordial.
Not marred, not so (I too, I should have said);
that darker but still blue distress
enriched the stone's peculiar price,
for blue naively blue, the lake
untampered by its island,
glib blue would make orfèvres yawn,
pensive, I too, I should have said.

But could this be? I came too late.
And yet I tried. My fingers held
that delicately irritated stone,
exquisite with sin, until
the symbol failed. "Am I," I heard
a child, a Jewess, whisper,
"the discord that beguiles the song?"

She was the flimsiest among the dead
and stinking innocently in a ditch.
A man had pushed that rod of his
between his legs between her legs.
Her skin slumped through her bones. She lay
in her own liquid filth licking
a piece of wood for succulence.
One morning she forgot her mother.
The winter froze two fingers off.
But milk and schoolsong recollections
kept her tough: she trusted God.
At last her turn she reached the ditch,

she knelt, was shot, fell blood to blood,
another's elbow slapped across her neck.

I trembled safe across an ocean.
Behind the barbed roses of Connecticut
El Sereno boomed his "all is well".
I could not find, oh Stevens, syntax
for this child, no jewel adequate,
no shape of nature that would tally
or be wholesome (since with rock
or thorn or tiger, symbol-making man
can anodyne his grief). And ever
untranscended, pain stands by,
there is no exile into peace;
still on my lips that excrement
successors will digest to art
but I must suffer brute and fat,
clotting paradise out of my voice.

[*Orfèvres*: makers and dealers of fine gold, silver and other precious objects, including jewels. *El Sereno*: a night-watchman in Spain. In the past, he also "boomed" the hours, adding, after the hour, "and all is quiet (sereno)".]

DO NOT PLACE YOUR TRUST IN BABIES

Do not place your trust in babies:
Himmler was one.
Remember he too took his first steps
on funny pudgy legs,
you should have seen him gurgle
and smile at the smiles he saw.
Ah what a happy family.

Next time you bend over a cradle
tuck a hatchet in your thoughts.

[This poem is effective only if the name in line 2 is immediately familiar. If it fails that test, why not replace Himmler with the name of a two-syllable human monster (trochaic or iambic) who is better known to a particular set or generation of readers? Why not "Nero was one"? I am in effect inventing here the genre of the *open-slot poem*, where the author permits the reader or editor to make a substitution for a given segment of a poem — a name or anything else. Another example: In the last line of the first poem in this volume, "An espresso at the 'Number Six'", Vitruvius could be replaced by Palladio, the difference in sound being immaterial. With this in mind, why didn't I use the names of Hitler or Stalin, which will remain far more familiar to the general public than that of the chief of the Gestapo? Something sinister in the sound of the "mm" led me on; perhaps, too, the wish not to be too obvious.]

ROBINSON JEFFERS:
"COME PEACE OR WAR, THE PROGRESS OF EUROPE AND AMERICA BECOMES A LONG PROCESS OF DETERIORATION."

What acreage has calamity
more than *I die*?
I died at maximum of Greece
before Protagoras disturbed its sky;
I died at England's best: Raleigh crossed the seas
but nothing was my destiny;
and in America's first dignity
and last, in spite of Jefferson's augustan eye,
I was obliged to die.

Let Europes and Americas abstractly rot.
Death occupies a smaller lot.

76

WORDS FOR JOHN STRACHEY'S "ON THE PREVENTION OF WAR"

John Strachey was his simple name.
In Britain rose his middling fame.

He thought of war. His manly spirit shook.
To kill off war he wrote a book.

The H bomb would exterminate us all.
Therefore (he reasoned) let it never fall.

John Strachey hoped that realistic negotiation
Would avert unthinkable obliteration.

We shall (he wrote) survive, if we agree
To shape a Super-Power World Authority.

Already he detected "a new attitude of mind."
With this the book came out and the reviews were kind.

But then he died. John Strachey, looking forward, died.
No H-bomb struck him; just the old foul-minded scythe.

Consider, John, our grievous lot:
Mankind survives, but men do not.

[John Strachey, author, Labour MP, and Secretary for War from 1950 to 1951.]

ON THE ASSASSINATION
OF PRESIDENT KENNEDY

1

First came the special issues of the magazines
With loyal photographs: the old rich times, the rocking chair,
The wife who knew who Dali is, the muscular war,
The politics retouched and smiling, the happy hammer
Of his power, the idiocy of death (at fifty cents).

The president was dead, tears fell and incomes rose.
Wait, brothers, wait,
My grief has gone to market too.

2

The picture books cost more but they were meant to last,
They used the most caressing words, like strong ideals
And dedicated heart and faith in our democracy.
And those who sold the plaster statuettes (one dollar each),
Their right hand mourned, their left rang up the cash.

The president was dead, laments and incomes rose.
Wait, brothers, wait,
My grief has gone to market too.

3

Congressmen deplored into the cameras, the voters saw
Their simple, manly sorrow. Foreign crowns were caught
Bowing usefully toward the great man's grave.
All were shocked; what's more they truly were; alas
One could not keep one's honest sobs untelevized.

The president was dead, tears fell and reputations rose.
Wait, brothers, wait,
My grief has gone to market too.

4

Next came recordings, and his voice was heard again
To make flesh creep from shore to shore. A publisher
Withdrew a luckless exposé of sin; a sensitive biography
Recouped the loss. Three journalists retold the terror
Irreversible. We shuddered, covered up our eyes, and bought.

The president was dead, laments and incomes rose.
Wait, brothers, wait,
My grief has gone to market too.

5

When great men breathe their last, their expiration
Swells our sails. Films shall be turned, sermons released,
Memoirs composed and statues erected. Pure grief is silent,
And yet pure fibbing is too hard for us. Our right hand
Wipes a tear, our left jingles the coins.

The president is dead; my poem goes to press.
Grief, brothers, grief
Is my profit, yet all the same I grieve.

[Shortly after the president was murdered in 1963, I was invited to contribute to an anthology of poetry about the assassination. It is the only commissioned poem I have ever written. The "profit", needless to say, resided entirely in the thought that a few people might be reading my equivocal elegy.]

HOW DID SAM BECKETT DIE?

How did Sam Beckett die?
Did he grin, or did he cry?

Done crooning all life long
How life's no better than a crock of dung,

Was he content to slither down the drain,
True to his pen and fame?

Or did he throw a tantrum, like the rest of us
Who seldom die without a fuss —

Bawling for another day, another hour,
Never mind, ah God, how caca sour?

Speak, scholars; I don't know. But I do find
Deep in my doggerel mind

That Art is sometimes *here* when Life is *there*:
Apple the one, the other pear.

"LATE FROST"
BY SUZUHIKO KAWASAKI

A girl who faces away,
A few loitering trees;
all stand alone
in the silver of snow.

The trees are nude and black.
Looking their way

has she guessed the old notion
that nowhere is home?

Notions stiff with age
stir when their masters call.
Snow shivers again, again
a child cries in a wood.

A girl, silver snow, four trees:
enigma warmer to me
than paint dropping from brush
to paint mere noises of paint.

[I purchased this large painting from the young artist in Tokyo during my
military service in 1954.]

BAD CHOICES

Reed. Born 1917 died 1985. Henry Reed.
No need

To prick your memory: Reed author of "Naming of Parts".
Wonderful poem. Each line, remember? starts

With rifle drill, then runs into a flower —
Nature so lovely, Man (no big surprise) an evil power.

Anthologies anthologies succeed,
Each picking ditto ditto by Henry Reed.

Hand me — thank you — that new collection —
Here, look: "Naming of Parts" — again the editor's "matured
    selection".

The thing, you understand, is most deserving,
And yet to print nothing but this I find unnerving.

You'll say, maybe our poet was delighted
To find his "Parts" so often reinvited.

I, however, see him tearing out his thinning hair,
Eyeing one more new collection with a baleful glare —

That poem again? I hate the sight of it.
My other verse — what is it? Tell me! Spit?

He banks his royalties — why not?
But wishes all anthologizers shot.

I grant I never knew the man; perhaps you disagree.
But now let's talk about unhappy me,

Who's less, much less, than Henry Reed.
No need

To prod your memory.
You never saw a line by me.

I've plagued my keyboard all in vain;
No couplet, triplet or quatrain

Of mine's in any Book of Modern Verse.
That too, you will agree, is quite a curse.

I tear my thinning hair
(And that's no guess — I vouch for it — I'm there);

From every pore that's in my soul I bleed.
But bleed I more than Henry Reed?

Not so, I say. My "fate" (forgive the pompous word)
Strikes me as of lesser hurt.

The reason, my good friend — let me explain — is very —
"Stop! I'm smart. No explanation necessary."

Four: Poems with animals

Upon noticing that animals play a role in a fair number of my poems, I decided to devote a "chapter" to poems-with-animals, ragardless (again) of their theme, form, tone, or period of composition. Indeed, some of them are very old, others quite fresh.

INSECT

The tiniest of wingless lives — a nervous atom —
aware of me bad giant, dashes for cover
under the Welcome mat on my kitchen floor.
Plenty of time to squash it: my big toe would do.
"Foul fleck, thou defilest my home!"
But I'm not of the killer breed.
The dot whisks under the mat: All clear!
Even insects, says Pity, are dear.

A FLY A FLY AND I

one fly that flies
one fly that drops,
neither content
nor not.

I do not wish
I were a fly;
I want to hate it
when I die.

MOTION

A worm lifts up a somber eye
And sees how sweet it is to fly;
What gossips, raids, impressions, climates, fun!
He's heard of flies that tango in the sun.

The fly (you guess the tale) admires the worm,
Enjoying on his decent inch the firm

Tradition of a twig. His own head aches
With every sprint he undertakes.

Eagles beg of moles a fling at sod.
God himself is bored with being God.
Why else did Zeus go slumming as a swan?
Why did the Holy Ghost go fooling as a man?

Cobalt atoms shiver in the very stone,
And dissolution is the amusement of bone.

I AM A LITTLE SNAIL

I am a little snail
in the green grass I sail
sometimes I live sometimes I die
and in between I hear great mankind cry
we mankind must survive
how ghastly to deprive
the cosmos of mankind
although the reason I can't find
being a little snail
in the green grass I sail.

AFTER LI PO

In a gentle silent pond
A jade pavilion stands;
Close by its door, among the fronds,
A bridge bows to the land.

And in the chamber sit
Three friends who drink warm tea;
They chat, and now and then they twit,
They chuckle when they disagree.

And in the gentle pond
A fish jumps at a fly.
The fly must stomach the affront.
No choice, the thing must die.

So still, so polished is the pond!
The house and bridge peep upside down,
And upside down the friends so fond,
The figured cups, the silken gowns.

But right side up and nothing else
The fish jumps at the fly.
The story which this story tells
No roguish mirror turns awry.

GARDEN IDYLL

Little brown bird, so very brown,
No blue, no red, no yellow on your gown,

Furtive at your nibbling like a fellow caught
Stealing something that he should have bought,

Welcome to the morning crumbs I threw,
Though I didn't mean them, I confess, for you —

I meant them for those jays that swoop
With royal screeching and a gallant loop

And don't so much as see you while you push
Your trodden presence underneath a bush.

Of singing not a hint, of whistling not a trace;
Just now and then a peep marks your disgrace.

You have, no doubt, a Latin name, but what's the point?
You're not the kind that Latin can anoint.

Nor would birdwatchers shiver in the ice of dawn
To train field-glasses at your prosy goings-on.

But eat, my lucky chum, grow fat: *you*'ll never know
How brown brown feels when others glow.

[The bird turned out, on inquiry, to be the brown towhee: *Pipilo crissalis*. This undistinguished family expelled the earlier residents of our garden, a family of jolly, impudent bluejays. For those interested in poetics, here is an instance where merely italicizing a word discloses the poem's theme.]

CROW

Yes you are as black as black is black.
So, soft to feel, are my lady's tresses.

You do not sing at all like an angel.
Deep Socrates harrumphed his lectures.

You are, I understand, carnivorous.
So very much am I.

Peasants called you bad luck and murdered you.
My bad luck has no need of birds.

Certain poets do not care for you.
I do not care for certain poets.

Come, you and kin, land in my garden
Any time for a bicker and a yarn!

I like smart company.

SLANTED BIRD

The unleafed branches of the tree in March
radiate, inverted parasol,
serious and quasi analytical.

That's when Nature plays the clown,
flies in and daubs a slanted bird
across a twig,

tousles the organization:
a whistle in a church,
a comma at the clause's end,

PIGEON FLY

What I hold in my hand here
is a pigeon all aflutter, though
were it whiter I should call it
dove, a syllable more promising.

I am hardly Noah as I lean
holding my pigeon at the window,
but since it's Spring and trees wake up
and flap their leaves: pigeon, fly!

It does not fly as elegantly
as in pictures I have seen;
still, it bears that little paper tube
tied round its ankle for my heirs.

How curious it will be, the day
one opens it and reads my hand.
"What made him send that stupid bird?"
I hoped you would be kind.

WHEN DOES WHY END?

When does why end?
Never.

Why is this?
Because of so.

Why is so?
Because of thus.

Why is thus?
Because of that.

Boundless mouse,
Unending cat.

HOMERIC SIMILE

Like a dog and his master:
both burly but of course the master burlier
still the dog tugs at the leash
the backward way he wants to go
where a bunch of mutts and pups are frolicking
and he wants to fool around with them
or bite their ears off
or pop a little sex
or just smell them under the tail
but the master is yanking oh yanking hard
and of course the master wins
but the dog has to be dragged
wrenched head bruised neck yelping
paws trenching four streaks in the gravel.
So mankind (you fill in the rest).

DEAD RATS

Lying on their flanks in our sweet garden —
hugging each other — two putrid rats —
"partners in life, united in death"
after they swallowed my green poison,
and already the flies, worms and other midget hyenas
are at work making omelets of them.

Somebody has to lift them into the bin.
I try with a shovel. No good. Damn damn.
They keep slithering off pell-mell.
I shove and dig and almost puke
knowing I'll have to use my hands.
It's their small revenge. Hate answers hate.

IMPATIENCE

Slow oxen hour, witless muddy animal,
I sit astride you
Shoving you with my buttocks,
I shout at you with the sweat in my face or
Beg you beg you to move with my best furious cajoleries
And then again give you a knock with my fist
        between your ears,
But nothing.
You take your insolent time.
I have to rejoice
You lift those paws of yours at all
And now and then we leave a tree behind.

[Impatience about what? If this poem were moved to its other rightful position, namely in the "Busy Eros" section right after "The Journey", the answer would be clear.]

A VISIT TO THE ZOO

I'll never see a camel in his orange desert,
Nor a parrot in a lurid Amazon.
That tigress knows it. I'm not worth her snarl.
I deserve that hugely unmomentous yawn.

THE YOUNG MAN WHO IS BLIND

The young man who is blind is smiling
While one reads the news to him.
He listens to the voice's voice,
Pretends an interest in the din.

And when one takes him for his walk,
The tramways kneel politely;
He smiles like canny Moses
Traversing the Red Sea.

The ice-cap melts, plutonium spills
And terrorists rap at my door.
He chats, he does not see
My blood washing the floor.

And all the peevish race sweats bread
Out of reluctant earth, but one
Comes feeding him, for which he smiles,
For he outwits the plan.

The wicked hate the wicked,
the kindlier hate the kind,
but he is evermore the lamb
in the lion's arms reclined.

Five: Tenebrae

Many of these poems of old age and extinction were written long before senescence set in. The young often feel old; the old seldom feel young.

THE KIDNEYS LAUGH AT PLATO

After running five minutes
I lie on the grass panting
And listen angry to my heart.

I want to call down the well of my body
"Organs, organs! Do you hear me? Discipline!"
Lord, to be dependent on a pancreas!

If it turns off I'm dead.
Do I choose to die? Not much!
Yet this fat machinery dares run me.

Salivating with indignation
I demand to be pure spirit,
I want to boss this heart, these kidneys, this tripe.

Did you, Plato, yes or no call them slaves?
Then why does that heart keep thumping
When I shout "At ease"?

ADRIANA IN SURGERY
(September 2007)

Death saw his chance. He made a dart
Into that gash two inches from her heart.

The surgeon bested him—stanched and sewed so well
The fiend went rolling back to Hell,

Sneering, though, *Arrivederci, bella* from his hole
To my wife's Italian soul,

And to my Belgian : *A bientôt, mon pote.*
Death the polyglot.

[Mon pote: pal!]

94

OPEN LETTER TO GOD

Sir, I've been looking up statistics.
Each 8 seconds a baby's born, each 20
1 wretch gets removed. Tick tock it goes.
I find, considering this exercise
In conclusionless logistics,
The come-and-go is useless. For, you see,
Life nicely wins, but death never loses.
Since we (next point) are quite as good
As Babylon or Komwatmay, stop birth, stop death,
Stick with us: it's good sense, it's even charity.
I add, being old, I think each day better
Of your creation, and shall be glad
To settle for good on your ground floor.

Thank you, Sir, for your attention to this letter.

THE SCHOOLYARD

Children at play
behind the school:
a laughing whirl,
merry misrule.

I watch them hard
my side of the fence.
I study the faces.
They make no sense.

Thirty years ago
I saw, I swear,
the self-same children
exulting there.

My hand on the fence
is pitted and pursed.
Why were they spared?
Why was I cursed?

OLD MAN IN LOVE

Never envy the young.
They are rivers
that won't flow without flooding,
they are magnates
who give to wrong charities,
and they fall with lamentable wounds
over a straw in an alley.

We are different:
sure as the hunter with a last bullet,
and the ice of his great hunger.

TO BLAISE PASCAL

Clever I have made a circle
and inside I stir my tea, ambition,
ladies, bank accounts and poetry,
and sophomoric erudition.

I keep as busy with my clutter
as a baby with his blocks,
I keep as busy as a sniffing
yapping hunting dog.

Keep busy is the rule of men
too shrewd to be too wise.
There is no horror in the air
until we realize.

[The allusion in the title is to Pascal's notion of *divertissements* — our busy
ways of averting our eyes from the abyss. The title of an earlier version of
the poem was "The Advantage of Trivia".]

ME FOR SOFT FLOORS

Me for soft floors and smartly not to think.
Vase at the window, carpet, couch, unopened books.
A lamppost on the asphalt, peeping through a tree,
Gives me a yellow, measurable wink.

I fear the moon, and fear the beauty and the stars.
Me keep me far from distance. They utter
My how dim I am how dumb I talk,
They light me naked up this mammal farce.

How can those nitwit lovers bear the sky?
Me for a chandelier hung not too high.

THE TREE

Somewhere I don't know where,
what kind, maybe in Minnesota,
there is a tree; "Good morning, dear,"
I say, "will it be really you,
you who sift the wind this province here

and whistle at your birds all's well?"
"Yes me; and is it really you,
with just two arms and still alive,
you with lips, you with eyes and legs
and whistling down to death oh well?"

There we met, we two, with great fine talk
of chance and how the atoms meet
with so much reason and no rhyme,
and how, though strangers now, we must
be staying longer in each other's arms
than me with Joan or he with jay.

And then I went my whistling way
Waiting waiting for the day.

MARCHING SONG

The dapper days are over,
  The dying must begin.
I was a crooked lover
  (nice song and mandolin)
but, customer of clover,
  I've reached the classic inn:
Wood for mattress, wood for cover
  on a rotten skin.
If only I could savor
  one last girl's first sin!
Then damn and die the rover:
  Eternity, you win.

GODLESS ON CHRISTMAS DAY

I hear the ancient churchbells swing
    and sow into the night
their charming seed, the Child,
    his promise and his might.

I hear them toll again, again,
    In dulci iubilo!
May only we who slaughtered him
    his dark departure know.

FORGIVE ME

Forgive me, you so pitifully dead,
when at the trombone's bleat I dance,
as I forgive, reluctant! in advance,
the whoopers on my grave and huggers in my bed.

THE PRISONER'S BALLAD

The prisoner falls down a ditch
and clutching at his pain he sighs
"I'll stop a bit." A soldier shoots,
the prisoner tips over, dies.

The soldier jumps into a hole,
an airplane sees him where he lies.
The bullets make a dotty line,
the soldier bleeds a pint and dies.

Home goes the pilot up the wind,
alas a shell bursts as he flies.
He thinks of mother, wife and child,
dives into the ground and dies.

Beside his head a daisy stands,
the night flings out its stars;
a blade of weed leaps round her stem,
the daisy chokes, death is no farce.

I rise and strut and din at God,
"Pity! Comfort! Bring release!"
God murmurs at the stars
"Continue, if you please".

MEMORIAL DAY

When you bring flowers to my grave
it won't occur to you, needless to say,
how degrading it is to be dead —
forced to accept "a loving tribute"
from my betters, you, mournful, erect.
You'll think, no doubt, "how grateful he would be
if he could speak," and hell I retch
thinking of me down there
mouth shut and mousy meek
six feet under a stupid violet.

ONE DAY, AFTER LUNCH

Coming downstairs
I saw that my wife, before driving to her yoga,
had sweetly left lunch on the counter for me.
There was a bit of fish left over from last night,
not bad if not exciting, the dwarf tomatoes
that made a near-bruschetta on my bread,
and radishes, because she knows I like them
with my toast and butter. The Pavoni, recently repaired,
made me a nice espresso, not far beneath
the famous coffee from the Tazza d'Oro.
Done, I stretched on the sofa in the den
for my customary doze, and there I slid,
snug, into my death: no doctors, no hospitals.

I had my wish.

MY FATHER: 1978

Eager to blame, I lift the past.
Let there be worms under the stone.
Like:
When I cried with exhaustion
you slapped me for making noise.
Or:
I wished to be a poet. You,
predictable merchant, fumed.
Or:
When they put me in uniform,
you said: It will make a man of you.

Or:
You blustered at the maids
but snivelled at the sight of any badge.
Or:
The week before you died
you took a fling at bankruptcy
hoping to defraud your creditors
six of whom were bosom friends.

Eager to blame, I lift the past.
I find no worms under the stone.
I can't hate down my grief. It grows.
                    Father!
Is it like you to hurt your child?

DEJECTION

A fishing-boat that was a boat
lists on the beach, slapped by wave or gale
across the hull till it groans and creaks.
Another plank drops in the sand;
one more nail or stud; some nameless
twist of cord. The sigh this adds
into the sum of things no man
no woman and no child appears
to hear, hear with a sigh. Seaweed
hears nothing, rock and shell are deaf.
An insect tunnels through his bit
of place. The moon appears. Or not.

IT

Let it die with me.
None need ever know.
Let it be erased.
It is better so.

Six: Torpors and Diminutions

Here are the allowed survivors (often revised) of far too many poems I have written on the topics of boredom, apathy, and insufficiency, although, to be sure, these are as capable of entertaining as any other.

PROFESSOR OSCAR MANDEL

I cannot build the house in which I thrive
Nor make the clever car I drive,

I haven't half a wretched clue
How mankind makes a bridge, a spoon, a shoe.

Merrily I jet to Paris
As stupid to its craft as any sack it carries.

Relaxed with cuddly wife and friends
I tweak the TV set, my science ends.

Like any monkey I can tweak and flick
And squeeze and press and twirl and click.

Things happen so a god would gape.
But why? But how? Go ask an ape.

Yet imbecile and talented I go,
Familiar, chipper, treading on your toe,

Blinking through the glasses I can't grind,
And glad to speak my parasitic mind.

MAN IS WHAT ANIMAL?

Chapter One

Man is the animal that laughs.

Chapter Two

Man is the only species warring on itself..

Chapter Three

Man is the animal that prays.

Chapter Four

Man is the cosmos become conscious of itself.

Chapter Five

Have you seen how endlessly and mellow
A cat lies on her pillow?

What have you done with us, my Lord?
Man is the animal that's bored.

[Upon revisiting this poem, I have my doubts about the perfect truth of some of its propositions, but a measure of truth surely remains.]

THE SWIMMER WITH THE LONG CIGAR

There was a man who jumped because he felt like it
    into the sea
off Florida (near Vero Beach) to swim he said to Tanezrouft.
They told him, those who knew, the place he named
    was far too far
and anyhow far in a continent far from the shore
and never had a drop of water dropped on Tanezrouft,
but "is that so?" said he and jumped into the sea,
guitar slung round his back and puffing at
    an eight inch long cigar.
Reporters say they saw him Tuesday noon doing the crawl
between Bou Djebeha and Abelbodh, chipper as a trout
for all the sand, "having furthermore acquired
the native patter and a rose-lipped slave to cool him
    with her fan."

Well! I too can swim! Teach me the rest, dear man.

THE LODGER
IN THE FLOATING ROOM

I am not in the export and import line,
nor in the professions; I am not
a computer engineer; and I am not
the man who lubricates your car.
I live in a small apartment
on the twenty-seventh floor except
there are no stories underneath at all.
I am quite detached (pardon the pun)
and do very little aside
from catching rain if it rains
with a butterfly net I stick out of my window.
Since the helicopters can't come
very near because of the blades
I will have to starve when the groceries
run out but all things considered
I am not in the export and import line,
nor in the professions; I am not
a computer engineer; and I am not
the man who lubricates your car.

THE PROOFREADER'S LAMENT

"Typewriters are cold enemies
To lions and the crickets in a chirping head"—
These were the words young Jason said
When he hankered for a golden fleece

And dropped a dungeon overboard.
And Byron was a gaudy heart, a rogue; in fine,
A baron with a nose for the sublime,

His day a fracas, and his night a sport.

Moreover, loonies there have been
Who climbed five flights into a leaking room
And therefore wove upon a loom
A sun, a zinnia, and a tangerine.

(A pencil on my thumb, I earn my keep,
Don't catch the moon, and look before I weep.)

[The word "Typewriters" rather than "Computers" (or any other electronic
device) dates this poem as "long ago".]

EASTER SUNDAY IN MY 28TH YEAR

In the tedium of my room all bulbs are lit
and stunned I attend to the walls
and sit.
I am mild as a sofa,
still as a vase, rooted in carpets.
Christ blew the shofar
and I saw tonight the first green pimples
on a shivering tree
and I came home shocked to be seen
in company with life.
I have had three experiences.
I want want. I am the antonym of knife.
Shall I learn gardening? Humus
under my fingernails might be amusing; I have heard
of snapdragons. Juvenes dum sumus.
At the outburst of the Resurrection
a man must cross naked into the light
and sing hosanna in a vertical direction.

I am not morally fit to die.
I must as yet enact
what muscles imply.

[*Gaudeamus igitur, Juvenes dum sumus*: So let us rejoice While we are young — the opening couplet of the well-known medieval Latin poem that became a student song.]

ON MY 29TH BIRTHDAY

Let's confer upon my elegy.
I'm twenty-nine, ah me, ah me.

Twenty-eight dear corpses, come near, come near.
I bring bad news for me to hear.

The price of glee is going up; please for a plan;
How shall I earn my chance to buy a little fun?

Twenty-seven, did you raise your metacarp?
Bone to bone, speak free, my friend, and sharp.

"You're a bore." But is that all? "No. Go hoard
Each dime of luck that you can swindle or extort,

Save, be humble, watch your health, and fast.
At ninety-two you'll be the laugher who laughed last."

I'll be the laugher who laughed least.
"Then shoot yourself. Some fools are never pleased."

THE ECSTASY OF BROTHER GILES

And Saint Bonaventure replied very earnestly
with his usual authority:
"Yes, the foolish old woman
is able to love God more dearly
than the doctor, and is indeed in some sense
the very heart of our theology."

Then Brother Giles ran into the garden
and then to the gate, past three
holy admirable birds and the blessed grass,
shouting and laughing many times between,
"Dumb silly peasant fool ho hey come here,
she loves God better than our Bonaventure!"

And immediately fell into an ecstasy
which lasted hours on the petunias
in front of the sky while I sat up
in my beachchair amazed
"He feels no inhibition before strangers,
But tears his breast open like a window
And sticks his heart out to the sun
And cries and cries and is so happy!"

Who bitter who invented facts?
Nothing since has made me even sad.

POOR AUGUSTULUS

If oh you wind had blown a whisper
Left or right of where you did,
I would have been a Kant, a Mozart,
Or more than Wilde in wit.

But while I flew, the way of leaves,
That secret wind went calm.
I dropped, I broke, my soul fell out,
Now I can do no good, no harm.

Who knows why great men bloom
And we the ninnies hush?
Who knows what wind brought Caesar,
And what Augustulus?

[Augustulus, Rome's inglorious last emperor, "an inoffensive youth" (Gibbon).]

SONG OF BOREDOM

A bird leaps up a tree,
   The clocks run after time,
The Senate spits a law
   against eternal crime,

Fresh factories go wild,
   There's so much progress on;
Idleness itself snores louder,
   and my lids fall down.

ALWAYS ALMOST

I loved you quaintly at the verge of a kiss.
Poet, the wind blew, went dull in July,
And dropped me in the sun. Nothing is complete.
I have no texts, only dull indices.

God wiped his mouth, nudged his dark Brother,
And said, pointing where Moses sweated:
"Show Moses the suburb of Palestine,
And shoot him at the border."

[This prophetic little poem is the first I ever published, namely in the *Georgia Review* as a page-filler in 1955. I have only slightly retouched it since.]

TRIPLETS

1

The world decreed me small,
If the world saw me at all.

2

Much and long I ran,
Ended, though, where I began.

3

Dwelling low,
Easy into earth I'll go.

Seven: The Poet

WHERE IS THE LIGHT?

Tell me, where is the light?
I'll after it
with gentle zeal
and modest adoration,
though it dangle off the ceiling
from a bulb
glowing dimly bright.

Better that than night.

SIR TOBY BELCH
AGAINST SHAKESPEARE

"William, William, tell me true,
What's the finest thing a man can do?"

Sow the verb and noun the earth,
Love the pen, and let the pen give birth.

"What of ladies and tycoons,
 Dogs and tennis, mayors and saloons?"

A lady is a trochee at her best,
A financier's an anapest,

The dog is half a foot,
And that's the use to which a dog is put.

"Farewell, grand master of the jingling craft,
Plato was no fool, who called you daft.

Your he she it what why and who
Get on and never think of you.

And I too swear no words can be
Better than a touchability.

So I'll choose love and drink and money,
And you go sing hey nonny nonny."

THE POET GROWS OLD,
IN FOUR MOVEMENTS

1

Like an old man who places
one foot before the other and worries
before he brings his other forward
before the first. So much for victory.
As for enthusiasms with regard to skies,
Fra Angelico, the touching bosoms of Saint-Tropez,
he hates three mammas who occupy his bench.

2

Time was, I launched asseverations.
I never thought but I encompassed.
I cried, five times a day: Oh!

3

The rhythms wobble and the words have quit.
My poetry must be desiring it.

4

The words are wobbling and the rhythms quit.
My poetry must be remembering it.

THE POET
IN A FOUL MOOD

What's it for anymore,
and what is it anyway —
this chopping off
of lines anywhere your genius decides,
and what's the point of it
since you same geniuses robbed it of meter
and shot rhyme, excuse me, rime dead?
Why not grouch and moan
in straight paragraphs
about your unspeakable dads and moms
and your suicides
and your rotten sex-lives
and what happiness it was to live
when the Ice Age was in bloom
and how utterly utterly
is the universe?
What's wrong with paragraphs?

I give up.
I mean I should.
Because I don't know how it happens,
but plop,
and eight months later,
plop,
a poem (I guess)
comes dripping out
my rotting spout.

THE POET
IN A HEAVENLY MOOD

I tiptoed on the daybreak of my genius
Saying to my very face Your Grace,

Tiptoed on the pinpoint of a blade
That spouted on the hill below the air,

One elbow on the sun and bussing
Winds to five incontinents,

Emitting jokes and raving holidays
And dating carnivals on Mondays —

Then it was the falcons turned herbivorous
And from a falling bomb mid-air

A chickadee came out and giggled
As it parachuted on a fainting general,

And I employed the idle Angels
And hollered the Dominions to the job

Of shooting roasts of pigeon to the poor
In Panama and Mexico —

Oh that was Sunday of my giant genius
And my name that Sunday was Your High

Serene Magnipotence and never
Sick Tom Fiddle with the wooden leg.

THE POET BECOMES
AN ASSISTANT PROFESSOR

Love I did, with tooth and tongue,
And sing I did, squalls of crotchets,
Blithe I lazed with tranquil eye,
Autumns flared and winters blazed,
And while their winds dissolved the trees
   I took the hours from a bonbonnière,
    And when the box was empty, found a spare.

But let me face the glorious facts:
Man is solid soul, he strives
To breathe with nostrils of a god,
He longs to task his deathless mind
And vaunt his distance from the beast.
   Besides, the lazy get no bread,
    And man must work in order to be fed.

The birdies fiddle sol mi do mi do.
But have they souls, the birdies? No.

[A *bonbonnière* is a box of sweets.]

A FELLOW POET IS RECEIVED
AT THE WHITE HOUSE

I was, one time, the chosen man.
I'd made a book: Is and Should, Chaos and Plan
Like Vulcan lame with rage
I banged into a shape upon a mighty page.

The Nation was (it happened) looking out
For an inspiring bard to boast about.
A president's assistant sent a note:
The busy chief desired to pin a medal on my coat.
I ran, I grinned, and had my photo snapped.
I spoke some loftitudes, the President looked rapt.
I lunched with senators and journalists.
I beamed each time my rump was kissed.
You laugh, Democritus, you laughing sage;
But ours is not the Periclean age.
And did you not yourself — in Greek — once say,
"When mules are mighty, lions bray"?

[The quote from Democritus (died c. 370 BC) is imaginary, as is of course
the whole episode.]

VARIOUS POETS

Some, scared of failure, don't even start,
I call that smart.

Some got loved, envied and hailed,
But wanting more, they think they failed.

Some, happy that they grew one green pea in a pod,
Sigh "Thanks be to God".

Some whose souls the halleluias rot,
Think they themselves are God.

Some whom the toughest saints would bless
Transmute to sweetness their success.

Some hammer at their shame
With blows of "Others are to blame!"

Some, inexhaustible at failing,
Keep up the hearty flailing.

Some hazard a last try,
Then, whispering "So be it", humbly die.

THE POET
FEELING SMALL

Ah to have been
A Cossack to cringing equations!

To have built
Majestic dams or interplanetary stations.

To have made
The genome bow, unpack and deliver.

To have proved
That Time was never never.

But then, to each of us his lot.
Mine, to fill a vacant slot:

One more lackey in "the realm of poetry."
Do re mi.

THE POET
WANTING FAME

Praise-me-praise-me! built the Parthenon
And peeled electrons shell by shell;
But who invented *praise-me-praise-me?*
Lucifer or Gabriel?

Grass rhymes selflessly with grass;
Winds, anonymous, mold cumuli.
Call it fair or call it foul:
Mankind made its bed and there I lie.

THE POET
NEITHER GUIBELLINE NOR GUELF

My pen you see roves little in the world,
my syllables are monks. For I perceive
that rhyming warm or cold won't hang a rascal
by the feet nor at the crisis shackle
any barking general. Mine the grief
that trails the earthworm to the hungry bird;
mine the minute dominion of the self:
dominion neither Guibelline nor Guelf.

THE POET GIVES UP

Le Roi Soleil struck down his man
by looking through his face
as though it were a spot of air
hung in a vacant space.

The world has done with me
entirely the same;
I could not even draw
the compliment of blame.

So into silence and farewell.
I'll never kiss
a word's lips with another rhyme.
The last be this.

Eight: Poems in French

Some of these poems appeared in my *Cette guêpe me regarde de travers* (Paris: Editions Bruno Doucey, 2010); others in the September 2013 issue of the *Gazette de la Lucarne*, a purely local newsletter printed by the Paris bookstore called La Lucarne des écrivains. These poems have no English equivalents, except for the first one, *Le Fou rêve de l'amoureux*, in which "The Garden" is given a new twist.

LE FOU RÊVE DE L'AMOUREUX

Je t'emmène vite vite dans un jardin
mais un jardin vingt fois
plus beau que paradis,
peuplé d'herbes inconnues en France
et de fleurs qui font pâlir nos parfums;
les moustiques y sirotent
le suc des pommes
et l'alouette dit à la grenouille
Que tu chantes bien !
dans mon jardin
vingt fois plus beau
que paradis.

Par dessus nos têtes un soleil couleur orange
engagé pour onze heures d'un matin
sans fin dans un mai sans trêve,
un nuage ou deux pour rire et des arbres
ah des arbres se démenant comme des fous
pour rester précisément sur place,
près naturellement de toi,
toi que leurs effrontés feuillages
abritent et espionnent.

Tout autour j'érige une muraille
épaisse, morose, faite d'une sale pierre rousse,
de la ferraille barbelée juchée dessus,
et ça et là un molosse pas content.
N'ayant pas d'ailes
j'y creuse un portail (un seul),
verrouillé d'un cadenas d'une tonne ou deux
dont la clé est dans ma poche.
Ce portail a de l'esprit car il comprend
que je suis concierge et roi.

Et après ? Ma langue s'en va.
L'heure de mon arrivée,
le bonjour que je reçois,
le poids et le contour de nos dialogues,
les baisers qui les sabotent
juste quand ils dépassent Socrate,
les rires que mon brave mur nous renvoie,
nos corps mouillés qui se tressent sur l'herbe —
rien, silence, aucune ambition
d'être un faiseur d'évangiles;
et chaque jour vient nous unir
la cloche d'une église lointaine
qui s'occupe d'autres que nous.

Et toi,
jamais tu ne me demanderas cette clé,
disant, ô si doucement, *Suffit !*
j'ai faim de la ville là-bas,
le bureau, la tante, les sous,
les choses qui se fânent,
jamais tu ne la prendras de ma main,
puisque ceux qui partent ne reviennent plus
plus jamais
dans mon jardin
ce jardin
vingt fois plus beau
que paradis.

HOULGATE

Je dis aux huit chevaux
qui trottent impeccablement sur la plage
tout au long du dernier murmure des vagues :
Votre beauté est étrange —
elle exista, elle existe,
hélas elle existera sans nous,
pourtant elle ne réjouit que nous,
car, derrière vos prunelles, dites, chevaux,
et dis-moi, chien qui les regarde passer,
où loge-t-il,
ce ah ! d'un être épris de beauté ?

L'AUTOBUS À PARIS
(le 25 juin 2004)

Tiens! Je suis un vieux bonhomme —
un vieillard, quoi !
Ça m'est arrivé d'un seul coup, sans préavis.

C'est pas vrai ? Je me trompe ?

Je te jure que je n'ai rien vu arriver.
Je regardais ailleurs.

Une femme, en plus pas très jeune,
m'offre son siège dans le 63.
Je crois rêver. Non, c'est bien moi qu'elle vise !

Tu veux savoir ce que je fais ?

Je fabrique un sourire qui me rend malade,
je m'assieds, je lui dis merci.

Salope, va !

OUI, VOUS AIMEZ LA NATURE

Oui, vous aimez la nature, c'est bien.
Moi non. Oui, quand même, parfois.
Regarder les boutons-d'or du pré me réjouit.
Et puis, ils ne font mal à personne
(que je sache). Mais la nature est méchante.
Elle a vingt crocs pour deux lèvres.
Ce n'est pas la peur qui fait trembler la terre !
et le coup de foudre qui attend le promeneur
n'a rien à voir, croyez-moi, avec l'amour.

SI JE POUVAIS

Si je pouvais mourir sans médecins,
Dieu! je t'inventerais
pour te dire merci merci bien !

NOTRE CATHÉDRALE

Les 100 coupoles de Rome
sont autant de bonnets.
bonnets dodus

bonnets assis
bonnets polis.

J'aime, moi, les flèches.
rapides
sans parenthèses
sans gras.

Je suis bon Anversois.

[The reference is to the cathedral of Antwerp with its magnificent spire.]

LES MORTS ONT PEUR

Les morts ont peur de mourir.
Ils nous disent :
    No sors pas ce matin, il fait froid.
    As-tu pris tes vitamines ?
    Serre la rampe quand tu descends.
    Que signifie cette tache ?
    Va, cours chez le médecin.
Car ils ont besoin de nous.
Je me souviens
Les sauve un peu du Rien.

CE QUI EST ARRIVÉ

Maman, j'étais loin quand tu es morte.
De l'autre côté de l'océan.
Et j'étais malade, c'est vrai.

Et mon passeport, je l'avais oublié
là-bas, encore plus loin.
Et d'autres obstacles….

Je les aurais bien foutus en l'air, salaud que je suis,
si on m'avait offert, à l'autre bout,
non pas ce cercueil,
mais un million.

LA MISÈRE

Rien n'a changé.
Les pauvres aux chemises trouées
puent encore de leur sueur.
Les enfants dont les mouches rongent les yeux
sucent toujours des tétons vides.
Quand le sol se tord les bâtiments qui croulent
broient trois riches et dix mille pauvres.
Les pauvres cueillent les tomates sous un soleil méchant
qui tuerait les riches.
Les pauvres cherchent du fil et des clous
dans les montagnes d'ordures.
Rien n'a changé.
Les pauvres rêvent de villas, de limousines,
rêvent de saigner les riches.
Sommés par les riches
les pauvres mitraillent les pauvres.
Éblouis par les brutes
les pauvres crient « Vive Hitler ! » « Hourra Pol Pot ! »
Rien ne change.
Dans un pli lointain de la galaxie,
un autre monde nous regarde, peut-être,
en n'en croit pas ses paisibles yeux.

SANS TITRE

J'ai mon domaine à moi,
J'y suis bien, car j'y suis roi.

Les autres rois sont bien plus grands,
Adulés de cent mille gens.

Mes cinq ou six me disent: « Que tu es fort ! »
Et s'ils n'avaient pas tort ?

Index to Titles

About the Author

Oscar Mandel is an acclaimed Belgian-born American author, scholar, and playwright who has published on numerous topics in English and French. He has written on the subjects of literary theory and art history, translated plays, and authored poetry, drama, and fiction. He is a professor emeritus of literature at the California Institute of Technology, having taught there for more than forty years. Learn more at oscarmandel.com.

Otherwise
FABLES

Oscar
MANDEL

CPSIA information can be obtained at www.ICGtesting.com
Printed in the USA
LVOW04n0908190515

439028LV00006B/36/P

9 781938 849558